What Comes Next? Logic Patterns

Math Books for Grade 1
Children's Math Books

Let's learn patterns so we will know what comes next!

Patterns

Patterns are things-numbers, shapes, images-that repeat in a logical way.

Patterns help us to learn to make predictions, to understand what comes next, to make logical connections, and to use reasoning skills.

Completing Pattern

Circle the picture that comes next in each picture.

Completing Pattern

Circle the picture that comes next in each picture.

Completing Pattern

Circle the picture that comes next in each picture.

Completing Pattern

Circle the picture that comes next in each picture.

Completing Pattern

Circle the picture that comes next in each picture.

Completing Pattern

Circle the picture that comes next in each picture.

Completing Pattern

Circle the picture that comes next in each picture.

Completing Pattern

Circle the picture that comes next in each picture.

Completing Pattern

Circle the picture that comes next in each picture.

Identifying Number Series

Identify the number pattern and fill in the missing numbers.

1. | 2 | 4 | 6 | 8 | 10 | |

2. | 17 | 19 | 21 | 23 | 25 | |

3. | 48 | 44 | 40 | 36 | 32 | |

4. | 10 | 15 | 20 | 25 | 30 | |

Identifying Number Series

Identify the number pattern and fill in the missing numbers.

5. | 27 | 25 | 23 | 21 | 19 | |

6. | 6 | 12 | 18 | 24 | 30 | |

7. | 1 | 3 | 5 | 7 | 9 | |

8. | 40 | 38 | 36 | 34 | 32 | |

Identifying Number Series

Identify the number pattern and fill in the missing numbers.

9. | 12 | 15 | 18 | 21 | 24 | |

10. | 32 | 30 | 28 | 24 | 22 | |

11. | 3 | 5 | 7 | 9 | 11 | |

12. | 22 | 20 | 18 | 16 | 14 | |

Identifying Number Series

Identify the number pattern and fill in the missing numbers.

13. | 5 | 10 | 15 | 20 | 25 | |

14. | 12 | 14 | 16 | 18 | 20 | |

15. | 77 | 70 | 63 | 56 | 49 | |

16. | 3 | 6 | 9 | 12 | 15 | |

Identifying Number Series

Identify the number pattern and fill in the missing numbers.

17. | 78 | 72 | 66 | 60 | 54 | |

18. | 27 | 29 | 31 | 33 | 35 | |

19. | 20 | 24 | 28 | 32 | 36 | |

20. | 39 | 36 | 33 | 30 | 27 | |

Identifying Number Series

Identify the number pattern and fill in the missing numbers.

21. | 55 | 50 | 45 | 40 | 35 | |

22. | 4 | 6 | 8 | 10 | 12 | |

23. | 26 | 24 | 22 | 20 | 18 | |

24. | 6 | 12 | 18 | 24 | 30 | |

Identifying Number Series

Identify the number pattern and fill in the missing numbers.

25. | 11 | 13 | 15 | 17 | 19 | |

26. | 64 | 60 | 56 | 52 | 48 | |

27. | 74 | 72 | 70 | 68 | 66 | |

28. | 10 | 15 | 20 | 25 | 30 | |

Identifying Number Series

Identify the number pattern and fill in the missing numbers.

29. | 48 | 45 | 42 | 39 | 36 | |

30. | 16 | 20 | 24 | 28 | 32 | |

31. | -11 | -9 | -7 | -5 | -3 | |

32. | 4 | 8 | 12 | 16 | 20 | |

Identifying Number Series

Identify the number pattern and fill in the missing numbers.

33. | 60 | 50 | 40 | 30 | 20 | |

34. | -24 | -22 | -20 | -18 | -16 | |

35. | 12 | 15 | 18 | 21 | 24 | |

36. | 25 | 20 | 15 | 10 | 5 | |

Identifying Number Series

Identify the number pattern and fill in the missing numbers.

37. | 62 | 64 | 66 | 68 | 70 | |

38. | -21 | -18 | -15 | -12 | -9 | |

39. | 6 | 12 | 18 | 24 | 30 | |

40. | 15 | 10 | 5 | 0 | -5 | |

Identifying Number Series

Identify the number pattern and fill in the missing numbers.

41. | 22 | 20 | 18 | 16 | 14 | |

42. | -5 | -3 | -1 | 1 | 3 | |

43. | 40 | 30 | 20 | 10 | 0 | |

44. | 14 | 16 | 18 | 20 | 22 | |

Identifying Number Series

Identify the number pattern and fill in the missing numbers.

45. | 96 | 88 | 80 | 72 | 64 | |

46. | -35 | -30 | -25 | -20 | -15 | |

47. | 13 | 11 | 9 | 7 | 5 | |

48. | 21 | 18 | 15 | 12 | 9 | |

Identifying Number Series

Identify the number pattern and fill in the missing numbers.

49.	7	14	21	28	35	

50.	-2	-4	-6	-8	-10	

51.	3	6	9	12	15	

52.	23	21	19	17	15	

Identifying Number Series

Identify the number pattern and fill in the missing numbers.

53. | -10 | -8 | -6 | -4 | -2 | |

54. | 5 | 10 | 15 | 20 | 25 | |

55. | 18 | 15 | 12 | 9 | 6 | |

56. | 32 | 36 | 40 | 44 | 48 | |

Identifying Number Series

Identify the number pattern and fill in the missing numbers.

57.

-10	-12	-14	-16	-18	

58.

84	77	70	63	56	

59.

-9	-6	-3	0	3	

60.

20	10	0	-10	-20	

Identifying Number Series

Identify the number pattern and fill in the missing numbers.

61. | 10 | 12 | 14 | 16 | 18 | |

62. | 25 | 27 | 29 | 31 | 33 | |

63. | 32 | 28 | 24 | 20 | 16 | |

Identifying Number Series

Identify the number pattern and fill in the missing numbers.

Count by 2 from 7 to 23

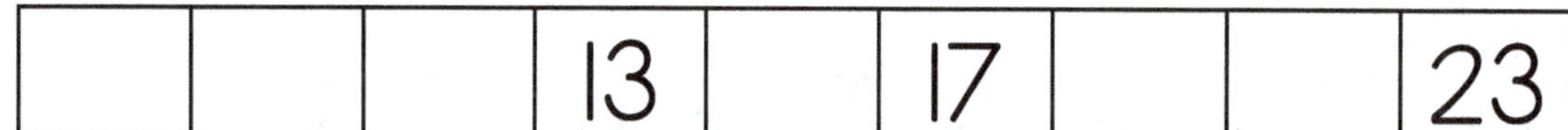

Count by 1 from 5 to 13

Identifying Number Series

Identify the number pattern and fill in the missing numbers.

Count by 2 from 1 to 17

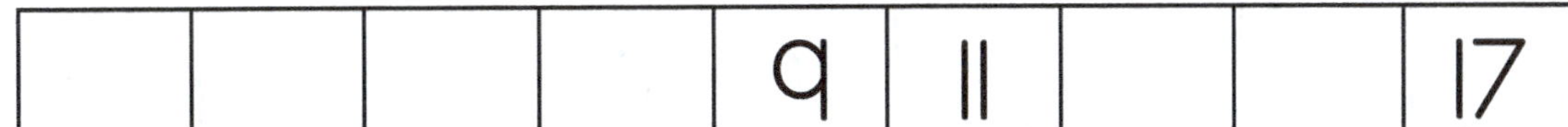

				9	11			17

Count by 1 from 3 to 11

	4		6	7				

Identifying Number Series

Identify the number pattern and fill in the missing numbers.

Count by 4 from 10 to 42

				26	30			42

Count by 3 from 7 to 31

				19			28	31

Identifying Number Series

Identify the number pattern and fill in the missing numbers.

Count by 1 from 6 to 14

		8	9			13	

Count by 5 from 6 to 46

6				31		46

Identifying Number Series

Identify the number pattern and fill in the missing numbers.

Count by 1 from 2 to 10

	3	4						10

Count by 2 from 10 to 26

10					22		26

Identifying Number Series

Identify the number pattern and fill in the missing numbers.

Count by 2 from 6 to 22

6	8			14			

Count by 3 from 4 to 28

4	7				22	

Identifying Number Series

Identify the number pattern and fill in the missing numbers.

Count by 4 from 7 to 39

7		15					39

Count by 1 from 5 to 13

				9	10		12	

Identifying Number Series

Identify the number pattern and fill in the missing numbers.

Count by 3 from 1 to 25

					16	19		25

Count by 2 from 1 to 17

		5				15	17

Identifying Number Series

Identify the number pattern and fill in the missing numbers.

Count by 1 from 48 to 41

	47			43		

Count by 3 from 43 to 22

			34		25	

Identifying Number Series

Identify the number pattern and fill in the missing numbers.

Count by 2 from 47 to 33

			41			35	

Count by 1 from 33 to 26

33						27	

Identifying Number Series

Identify the number pattern and fill in the missing numbers.

Count by 1 from 42 to 35

		40				35

Count by 3 from 45 to 24

			36			24

Identifying Number Series

Identify the number pattern and fill in the missing numbers.

Count by 1 from 35 to 28

	34		32				

Count by 2 from 45 to 31

	43			37			

Answer keys

Completing Pattern

Circle the picture that comes next in each picture.

Completing Pattern

Circle the picture that comes next in each picture.

Completing Pattern

Circle the picture that comes next in each picture.

Completing Pattern

Circle the picture that comes next in each picture.

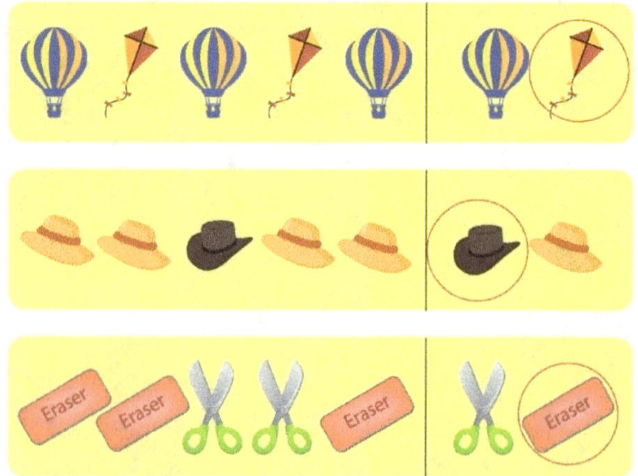

Completing Pattern

Circle the picture that comes next in each picture.

Completing Pattern

Circle the picture that comes next in each picture.

Completing Pattern

Circle the picture that comes next in each picture.

Completing Pattern

Circle the picture that comes next in each picture.

Completing Pattern

Circle the picture that comes next in each picture.

Identifying Number Series

Identify the number pattern and fill in the missing numbers.

1. | 2 | 4 | 6 | 8 | 10 | 2 |

2. | 17 | 19 | 21 | 23 | 25 | 27 |

3. | 48 | 44 | 40 | 36 | 32 | 28 |

4. | 10 | 15 | 20 | 25 | 30 | 35 |

Identifying Number Series

Identify the number pattern and fill in the missing numbers.

5. | 27 | 25 | 23 | 21 | 19 | 17 |

6. | 6 | 12 | 18 | 24 | 30 | 36 |

7. | 1 | 3 | 5 | 7 | 9 | 11 |

8. | 40 | 38 | 36 | 34 | 32 | 30 |

Identifying Number Series

Identify the number pattern and fill in the missing numbers.

9. | 12 | 15 | 18 | 21 | 24 | 27 |

10. | 32 | 30 | 28 | 24 | 22 | 20 |

11. | 3 | 5 | 7 | 9 | 11 | 13 |

12. | 22 | 20 | 18 | 16 | 14 | 12 |

Identifying Number Series

Identify the number pattern and fill in the missing numbers.

13. | 5 | 10 | 15 | 20 | 25 | 30 |

14. | 12 | 14 | 16 | 18 | 20 | 22 |

15. | 77 | 70 | 63 | 56 | 49 | 42 |

16. | 3 | 6 | 9 | 12 | 15 | 18 |

Identifying Number Series

Identify the number pattern and fill in the missing numbers.

17. | 78 | 72 | 66 | 60 | 54 | 48 |

18. | 27 | 29 | 31 | 33 | 35 | 37 |

19. | 20 | 24 | 28 | 32 | 36 | 40 |

20. | 39 | 36 | 33 | 30 | 27 | 24 |

Identifying Number Series

Identify the number pattern and fill in the missing numbers.

21. | 55 | 50 | 45 | 40 | 35 | 30 |

22. | 4 | 6 | 8 | 10 | 12 | 14 |

23. | 26 | 24 | 22 | 20 | 18 | 16 |

24. | 6 | 12 | 18 | 24 | 30 | 36 |

Identifying Number Series

Identify the number pattern and fill in the missing numbers.

25. | 11 | 13 | 15 | 17 | 19 | 21 |

26. | 64 | 60 | 56 | 52 | 48 | 44 |

27. | 74 | 72 | 70 | 68 | 66 | 64 |

28. | 10 | 15 | 20 | 25 | 30 | 35 |

Identifying Number Series

Identify the number pattern and fill in the missing numbers.

| 29. | 48 | 45 | 42 | 39 | 36 | 33 |

| 30. | 16 | 20 | 24 | 28 | 32 | 36 |

| 31. | -11 | -9 | -7 | -5 | -3 | -1 |

| 32. | 4 | 8 | 12 | 16 | 20 | 24 |

Identifying Number Series

Identify the number pattern and fill in the missing numbers.

| 33. | 60 | 50 | 40 | 30 | 20 | 10 |

| 34. | -24 | -22 | -20 | -18 | -16 | -14 |

| 35. | 12 | 15 | 18 | 21 | 24 | 27 |

| 36. | 25 | 20 | 15 | 10 | 5 | 0 |

Identifying Number Series

Identify the number pattern and fill in the missing numbers.

37. | 62 | 64 | 66 | 68 | 70 | 72 |

38. | -21 | -18 | -15 | -12 | -9 | -6 |

39. | 6 | 12 | 18 | 24 | 30 | 36 |

40. | 15 | 10 | 5 | 0 | -5 | -10 |

Identifying Number Series

Identify the number pattern and fill in the missing numbers.

41. | 22 | 20 | 18 | 16 | 14 | 12 |

42. | -5 | -3 | -1 | 1 | 3 | 5 |

43. | 40 | 30 | 20 | 10 | 0 | -10 |

44. | 14 | 16 | 18 | 20 | 22 | 24 |

Identifying Number Series

Identify the number pattern and fill in the missing numbers.

45. | 96 | 88 | 80 | 72 | 64 | 56 |

46. | -35 | -30 | -25 | -20 | -15 | -10 |

47. | 13 | 11 | 9 | 7 | 5 | 3 |

48. | 21 | 18 | 15 | 12 | 9 | 6 |

Identifying Number Series

Identify the number pattern and fill in the missing numbers.

49. | 7 | 14 | 21 | 28 | 35 | 42 |

50. | -2 | -4 | -6 | -8 | -10 | -12 |

51. | 3 | 6 | 9 | 12 | 15 | 18 |

52. | 23 | 21 | 19 | 17 | 15 | 13 |

Identifying Number Series

Identify the number pattern and fill in the missing numbers.

53. | -10 | -8 | -6 | -4 | -2 | 0 |

54. | 5 | 10 | 15 | 20 | 25 | 30 |

55. | 18 | 15 | 12 | 9 | 6 | 3 |

56. | 32 | 36 | 40 | 44 | 48 | 52 |

Identifying Number Series

Identify the number pattern and fill in the missing numbers.

57. | -10 | -12 | -14 | -16 | -18 | -20 |

58. | 84 | 77 | 70 | 63 | 56 | 49 |

59. | -9 | -6 | -3 | 0 | 3 | 6 |

60. | 20 | 10 | 0 | -10 | -20 | -30 |

Identifying Number Series

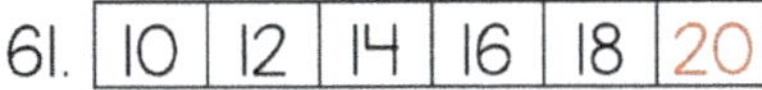

Identify the number pattern and fill in the missing numbers.

61. | 10 | 12 | 14 | 16 | 18 | 20 |

62. | 25 | 27 | 29 | 31 | 33 | 35 |

63. | 32 | 28 | 24 | 20 | 16 | 12 |

64. | 30 | 35 | 40 | 45 | 50 | 55 |

Identifying Number Series

Identify the number pattern and fill in the missing numbers.

Count by 2 from 7 to 23

| 7 | 9 | 11 | 13 | 15 | 17 | 19 | 21 | 23 |

Count by 1 from 5 to 13

| 5 | 6 | 7 | 8 | 9 | 10 | 11 | 12 | 13 |

Identifying Number Series

Identify the number pattern and fill in the missing numbers.

Count by 2 from 1 to 17

| 1 | 3 | 5 | 7 | 9 | 11 | 13 | 15 | 17 |

Count by 1 from 3 to 11

| 3 | 4 | 5 | 6 | 7 | 8 | 9 | 10 | 11 |

Identifying Number Series

Identify the number pattern and fill in the missing numbers.

Count by 4 from 10 to 42

| 10 | 14 | 18 | 22 | 26 | 30 | 34 | 38 | 42 |

Count by 3 from 7 to 31

| 7 | 10 | 13 | 16 | 19 | 22 | 25 | 28 | 31 |

Identifying Number Series

Identify the number pattern and fill in the missing numbers.

Count by 1 from 6 to 14

| 6 | 7 | 8 | 9 | 10 | 11 | 12 | 13 | 14 |

Count by 5 from 6 to 46

| 6 | 11 | 16 | 21 | 26 | 31 | 36 | 41 | 46 |

Identifying Number Series

Identify the number pattern and fill in the missing numbers.

Count by 1 from 2 to 10

| 2 | 3 | 4 | 5 | 6 | 7 | 8 | 9 | 10 |

Count by 2 from 10 to 26

| 10 | 12 | 14 | 16 | 18 | 20 | 22 | 24 | 26 |

Identifying Number Series

Identify the number pattern and fill in the missing numbers.

Count by 2 from 6 to 22

6	8	10	12	14	16	18	20	22

Count by 3 from 4 to 28

4	7	10	13	16	19	22	25	28

Identifying Number Series

Identify the number pattern and fill in the missing numbers.

Count by 4 from 7 to 39

7	11	15	19	23	27	31	35	39

Count by 1 from 5 to 13

5	6	7	8	9	10	11	12	13

Identifying Number Series

Identify the number pattern and fill in the missing numbers.

Count by 3 from 1 to 25

1	4	7	10	13	16	19	22	25

Count by 2 from 1 to 17

1	3	5	7	9	11	13	15	17

Identifying Number Series

Identify the number pattern and fill in the missing numbers.

Count by 1 from 48 to 41

48	47	46	45	44	43	42	41

Count by 3 from 43 to 22

43	40	37	34	31	28	25	22

Identifying Number Series

Identify the number pattern and fill in the missing numbers.

Count by 2 from 47 to 33

47	45	43	41	39	37	35	33

Count by 1 from 33 to 26

33	32	31	30	29	28	27	26

Identifying Number Series

Identify the number pattern and fill in the missing numbers.

Count by 1 from 42 to 35

42	41	40	39	38	37	36	35

Count by 3 from 45 to 24

45	42	39	36	33	30	27	24

Identifying Number Series

Identify the number pattern and fill in the missing numbers.

Count by 1 from 35 to 28

35	34	33	32	31	30	29	28

Count by 2 from 45 to 31

45	43	41	39	37	35	33	31

Visit
BABY PROFESSOR
EDUCATION KIDS
www.BabyProfessorBooks.com
to download Free Baby Professor eBooks
and view our catalog of new and exciting
Children's Books